Death Meditation

Simon Davies

LeftHandPress
A Division of Black Moon Publishing, LLC
New Orleans, Louisiana USA

Format Copyright © 2016 Left Hand Press
A division of Black Moon Publishing, LLC

LeftHandPress.com

Design and layout by
Jo Bounds of Black Moon Publishing

Editor's Note

This is an original manuscript submitted to the Black Moon Archives circa 1980's. The text published here is as originally submitted and reflects the masculine tone concerning gender as was common at the time.

ISBN: 978-0692812013

United States • United Kingdom • Europe • Australia • India

CONTENTS

To Caroline

BIRTHWORD

This small book is not a treatise on death, but rather a short study of death and the various ways we experience death. It also contains information about how we view death and the Gods, Goddesses and Worlds which we have created for the embodiment of death.

Death is no stranger. We experience death constantly, day in and day out; our body is in a permanent state of decay and rebirth. There lies the lesson. Death has fear only for those who cannot see and will not experience it. For those with eyes to see, they will perceive that death is followed by rebirth. It is not the fear of physical demise which is worrying, but rather the fear of the ego becoming extinct. Search out the soul, the soul beyond ego and death and you will discover the secret behind initiation. To experience death is to experience life; for, to those who see, both death and life are the same, two sides of the same coin.

The Dark Night of the Soul is followed by the Bright Day of Truth . . .

Seek death and birth will come in its wake . . .

DEATH

"Against his will he dieth that hath not learned to die. Learn to die and thou shalt learn to live, for there shall none learn to live that hath not learned to die."
   – Tibetan Book of the Dead, trans. by Dr. W.Y. Evans-Wentz.

"There, you are virtually nothing. A hundred years from now you will be a handful of dust, and that will be for real. All right now, act on that reality. And out of that . . . nothing. You will suddenly surprise yourself: The more you know you are nothing the more you will amount to something." – Death, Alan Watts.

Death is the end of all, that is how we view it in our day to day existence. Yet it is not the end, not in reality, for those who have learnt to die will live once more; they will die again in birth. Birth and death are synonymous in the experiential sense. Death is an unknown, so is birth; birth is a painful and traumatic experience, being flung into the unknown and ever light world of what we call reality. Death too is a traumatic experience, we do not know what lies behind its gate, it scares us that we don't know. Yet are animals afraid to die? They know not what death is or even if it exists for them, they fear it not for it is not known or unknown.

"It has been said that Death came into existence only with the rise of man's consciousness, a roundabout way of saying death is more real for humans than for any other animal, because only humans foresee it. Religions owe their existence to the unique ability of the human animal to understand that it must die." We see here that not only is man the only animal to understand that it must die but also that religion is totally based upon death; and of course the fundamental belief in the soul as the survivor of this experience. Religion not only teaches in their doctrine an after-life but also that life is eternal and never-ending. Most religions at one time or another have believed in rebirth, that is reincarnation. It is fundamental in the rebirth tradition for it gives man a chance to have a moral code and to expiate any 'badness' which he may have incurred upon himself. This of course is the belief in Karma, not only Eastern, but rather a world-wide belief wherever rebirth is taught.

The common attitude towards death in our present age is one of fear, it is a fear of the unknown. Man must always have his life mapped out, he must know what is coming next and have the ability to eradicate any uncertainties which enter the equation. This manner is not only wasteful but leads to Man becoming overawed by the thought of such a certainty as death. We all come into life with the same chances of immortality in flesh – none. We know that we will die yet we do nothing about it but rather obscure this rather irritating uncertainty from our minds. Eventually though it comes; some turn to religion in a last hope that there may be something, while others think of what they could have done and how they have wasted their lives. To eradicate the uncertainty we therefore, if wise, turn to religion in our early life. This is the hope, it is the illusion of certainty which religion contains that gives us the impetus to join. Once there however, people don't use it for that which it was designed. It was designed for the experience of death and in that, and only that, comes the certainty.

The religious orders, if true, should give a system of soul-release, common in the shaman's 'magical flight of the soul'. This in itself is an experience of the soul, that which is the immortal within us all. In these ecstatic trances man comes to experience a plane of wonder and a different reality, he comes to see that there are more levels to the same spectrum than he at first thought. This experience, whether fully ecstatic or just revelationary, gives the postulant something which is out of the normal consciousness of day to day reality and something which is of another world – death. The experience of death is not the common view of stillness and unthought, but rather one which is dreamlike and vivid, not what we would call 'dead' at all! Religion, and the accepting and following of a religious structure, is in itself an acknowledgement of death. We are accepting the inevitable and doing our best to prepare for it.

So religion can be seen to have been created from man's consciousness of things ending, or rather of his uncertainty of future existence. Yet even within the religious structure comes an image which is not at all likeable to the human living in the bright world. The concept of death is rather one of darkness and coldness. The funerary clothes are dark as is the mourner's dress. It is a solemn occasion, seen as the permanent ending of someone's life, never again to live. This is religion. This is the unreligious religion. Death is not frightful and dark but rather this is the uneducated view of it. These symbols represent the unknown and are therefore used by the unknowing. Llke the night in which we cannot see, so the uncertainty of death is likened to the night as if we cannot see. But we can see through the darkness, that is what the death experience is all about. The outer images shown to common man of the darkness are initiatory tests as it were; man must delve behind them and discover the death-rebirth aspect. For if we view one side of the coin, that of the 'unknown-beyond-death' and not the other of 'rebirth-beyond-death' then we are seeing only half of a reality. Death is not the end of the existence of Joe Bloggs, for he lives in all whose lives he touched and in whose memories he lingers on. What that man/woman did in that life is important and is to be remembered, that is part of their eternal existence, their immortality in the physical world.

But what then is the function of death if man is, in reality, immortal and ever-living? It is the change which is seen in all life in one way or another. All things must change and be reborn afresh. The old make way for the young and likewise the old themselves once more become young. Death is the natural 'spring-clean', it renews and rejuvenates. Alan Watts sees it as the natural method of renewing the memory once it has become full of experiences. We start again and relive, under different circumstances, life once more. The whole universe can be seen as this on/off, on/off system. This system is that of creation and destruction and then the final destruction and the initial creation once more. We find this greater death and rebirth of life as a whole in almost all belief systems. There is the initial creation and the final destruction, yet after, there is again another initial creation and once more a universal destruction. We can see this in the human body; the cells are constantly dying and being replenished throughout life, the final dissolution being death. Yet even this is not final, the body breaks down and feeds the ecological system, this gives rise to new life and aids that which is already in existence.

The earth, too, can be seen as a living organism. All that lives off her dies and goes back to where it came from, back to the mother.

She is the giant system from which we have come and unto which we shall go to after death. This system is, or can be seen to be, a set of controls. The earth is very sensitive and small alterations in its body chemistry cause changes to occur. The previous lives of such animals as the dinosaur was cut short when a chemical change occured in the body of the Goddess as Earth. It was a time of rest, a time between lives in which to gather together strength and forget the memories of that previous life. Once more the earth opened its doors and life again sprung up, this time though, I think the earth may have created something which may be the final blow. Perhaps we have overtaken the body like a disease which will eventually destroy its host. If we do end, it will not be known whether or not life will again come to this fair land; all we can do is hope and pray that man sees the errors of his ways and stops the cancerous growth before it goes too far – if it has not already done so!

Man, as an individual can be seen to be the same being, we too must watch ourselves and understand that death is a necessary change, in whatever form it comes.

Rebirth is the teaching within religion which helps us to see a light in the darkness of the unknown. Rebirth is the theme which joins together all the loose strands in the complex of death and presents it as a workable system. That it exists and has been experienced is plain to see. Almost all beliefs have it as a doctrine. Caesar said the Druids believed in the theory of cyclic return. The after-worlds of most cultures see a return to the living. *The Tibetan Book of the Dead* is a prime example, both of the belief in life-after-death and the cycle of return. Within this theory, as mentioned before, is the belief in the, soul. This too, is world-wide.

The rebirth theory is also enmeshed within the complex matrix of the Goddess. She is the visual diety of birth and death. She, as the Triple-Goddess is the being which man has exemplified as the beginning and the end; the womb and the tomb. That man saw her as the womb and tomb is also very clear. Pagan man was buried in the ground, the womb of the mother, or else he was placed in a womb-shaped barrow or grave, usually in the fetal position of birth. That this same man saw rebirth is signified by the spiral markings which usually inhabit these barrow or mound graves. This is one of the primal symbols of man and is taken to be the sign of cyclic return and the theory of the after-life.

This same symbol was later seen in the swastika which has a motive and everchanging quality about it – like the wind perhaps!

The Goddess as the beginning and end, birth and death is seen as her three stations, often compared to the Moon's cycles. Here she is seen as the creator, preserver and destroyer. This can be seen again in almost all faiths. In the Irish pagan system she was the Morrigan (Ana, the virgin, Badb the 'boiling' mother and Macha, the Mother Death), to the Norse she was the Norns (Urth as the virgin fate, Verthandi the mother being and Skuld or Skadi as the death-mother of necessity), to the Greek she was the Moirai (Clotho the spinner of Man's fate, Lachesis the measurer of a man's life and Atropos who was the cutter of a man's fate), we also find this image in the Celtic Arthurian legends (Elaine – Morgawse – Morgan). The Indian Kali-Ma was also a trinity but usually seen as a singular aspect of the darkness of death, blood being the main offering in her temples. Black Annis is the English equivalent to the death aspect and Goddesses such as Hecate, the Irish Cailleach and others are this very same death aspect.

The dark side of the Mother Goddess in her triform complex is usually seen to be dark coloured, black or blue, with an eye in the centre of the forehead and waving a knife in readiness for the next victim. All, though, are assured to meet this dark Goddess when they die, she is unavoidable. Though this Goddess has a horrible image, she is visualized and much used as the primal Goddess, for both birth and death, as we saw earlier, are synonymous. Therefore the Goddess as death is only dark to the mind that does not perceive; to those with wisdom or meditational ability, she is the light at the end of the dark tunnel of the unknown. For that which gives us life at birth also gives us life at death, she is the everpresent gateway in and out of physical form. So in this form the wise use as the centre of creation and destruction, not only of man but also of the Gods. The triple aspect of the fates in all their cultures are seen to be older than the oldest God, they created the Gods and planned their fates, as they also are seen to plan Man's fate.

It is because of this aspect of the Goddess, which is found in most cultures, that we have such rites as the Tibetan chod (to be dealt with later) in which the focus is death and the terrible Goddess, who is also the most popular. We find those, especially amongst the pagan fraternity, who worship only the light self of the Goddesses, seeing here the life of beauty and calm. Yet, to see into the third eye of Kali is to see the most wondered of all life, to see that death is in reality only the continuance of life and therefore something which is above all else.

This image is found in connection with many pagan beliefs. The witches worshipped her in the graveyards; this connection has come down to the modern conception of the witch as hag and death, an evil-doer. Death vigils and the ritual use of graveyards are common throughout history. The place of the dead, and indeed the spirits of the ancestors were all important. Death was as important a time, if not more important, as birth and was given great ritual significance. The death theme can be carried on once more with the image of Kali. Her worship by sacrifice was the decapitation of the sacrificial animal. This was so common that her temples were in fact seen as a slaughterhouse. This image of blood (as life) and the Goddess Kali is again carried forward by Barbara Walker, "Kali was the Ocean of Blood at the beginning and the end of the world, and her ultimate destruction was prefigured by destruction of each individual, though her karmic wheel always brought reincarnation".

The connection between the crone Goddess of the trinity and blood and death are unmistakable. But likewise she is also the wheel of karmic rebirth, and that of destruction for creation. As Barbara Walker says, she is both the beginning and the end – and we can surmise, the beginning after the end.

The Goddess was not the only figure which the mind of man saw as being representative of death. The God too, was an angel of death and a ruler of the world of the dead – the Underworld. The first God was perhaps the Hunting and Horned God. This was seen in the guise of a wild man, a man wearing antlers (as in the French cave drawings or the Cernunnos figures) or a stag itself. The Gods as the Horned God were common and specifically associated with death, not only the death of the hunted animal, but also the death of man himself. The primal vision of the Mother Goddess as creatrix and destructor was now partnered by the God. He was seen perhaps as her own dark self, she could be concentrated upon as the bringer of life to the womb whilst he was seen as death, the great changer.

The Christian devil is the prime example of the God as the horned image of death. Although made up of all the pagan images of the horned God the devil comes through in the Christian mythologem as the evil side of life. He is not however, evil, but was also, like the Goddess, also the preserver. He was seen both as the supplier of meat in the winter and also the taker-away of the weak in winter.

The God too was seen to be a triform God as was the Goddess. He too had the common image of creator, preserver and destroyer. As this triform aspect he paralleled the Goddess; in fact it has been suggested that he only had these three aspects so that he could partner the Goddess. He was above all a sacrificial God and in this role he illustrated the theme of rebirth. He was sacrificed as the stag-God in the later agricultural times at May-day as the sower of the seed. Later on in the year he was the crop and sacrificed to the people. So we see him as sacrificing himself to the Goddess, the dominant and ever-present deity. The sacrificial theme went on from the days of hunting, through the fertility of cattle and crops to the astrological Gods of the Sun and Moon. The solar hero is nearly always sacrificed, as was the divine king to the land. Christ, Lugh, and Osiris are all Gods of solar and sacrificial themes, and all are connected with the knowledge of death and the Goddess. Jesus is buried in a cave, a symbol of the Underworld and the womb of the Earth Goddess. From this at his resurrection he gained the knowledge of death and was therefore all-wise, all was known for the great unknown had been conquered. Osiris too, is killed by his brother Set and resurrected by the Goddess Isis. His son Horus then takes revenge and kills Set. The child is the divine starchild as rebirth through the Goddess at Yule. Lugh too, in the Celtic myth, is beaten by his evil alter-ego Gronw. He goes in the form of an eagle (a common conception of the soul) to Cerridwen (a white sow) the queen of Death. He is later resurrected to take revenge on Gronw, the husband to Cerridwen and Lord of Misrule and Death.

The two images of God and Goddess go together to portray an image of death and rebirth. They are nowhere better illustrated than in the pagan myths and legends of times past. Yet their images linger on in the modern cults like Christianity. The male God cannot offer rebirth, this is fundamental, even to the soul's rebirth in heaven, and therefore a totally male religion is incomplete. There must be the mother figure to present the rebirth and life eternal. Hence in the later Christian doctrines the Goddess of Chaos is removed and so was the complimentary teaching of rebirth.

As the God of the Underworld, the God is seen as ruler but not really as a transformer. The Goddess is the image of death and transformer. The God is merely there as the guardian and host of the dead. Hades is such a God, sitting in his halls ruling over the dead. His wife is the Phantom Queen of the Underworld, Persephone, daughter to the Earth Goddess Demeter. It is Persephone, as the other side of the image of Demeter who is the transformer of the dead. It is she who descends to the Underworld for three months a year to cause death in the land. It is she who brings the image of death to the people.

So if we reflect back we have a view which shows that the Goddess as seen by Man for death is dark and fearsome. Yet when preceived and looked upon she becomes the lighter side of rebirth and the necessary death, making room for new birth. She is the cleaner of the land and its people. The God as her consort is the emblem of death, he is the sacrificial victim to her and life, and he represents, in the myths, the image of rebirth through the Goddess as the divine child. What we get from this is a system of man's portrayal of death and rebirth in nature, not only of himself but of all that exists.

As hunter of the souls the God appears as Herne the hunter, the Stag-God of the Windsor woods. He is seen hunting with the spectral white-and-red-eared hounds with a host of souls. It is to the soul that we now turn and to the religious view of life after death. The Goddess in particular was an image which was to have been presented before this as it is she who is man's image of death and how he views it. Now we will look upon man's view of himself as eternal.

Man's view of the soul has been taken from the initial pagan beliefs which go back to man's first contemplation of the Mother as birth and later as death. Man obviously disintegrated and went into the earth and hence his image was the Goddess as Earth. But he must have seen that if man were to survive death it was in something invisible, in the world of dreams which occurred in his sleep, those imaginative tales which faded quickly upon his waking. So he thought, and rightly so, that the soul was within and without of his being. It was the air that surrounded him, that of which all alive partook; not only man but the animals and the plants. The air was his life, if he held his breath he would fall asleep in a faint, the life was contained in the air. Not only was his soul air but the power of life (spirit) was also air. When man died he stopped breathing, his soul had gone back to the Great Soul, seen as the air. Likewise when he slept his soul left his body.

Sleep is seen as a small death, and the primitive pagan people would have seen sleep and it's images as death and the afterworld. The shamanic trance (which we shall examine later) was also likened to a death. Man must die temporarily to visit the world of the dead and that of the Gods. Sleep and dreams were therefore seen to be real representations of the dead world and meditational trances were a conscious visiting of this world. As we shall see later it is the knowledge of death which gives man power over it and the freedom from the unknown. This in turn leads to the man being free from uncertainties in life, hence he can be at peace. This is what this book is about – about showing what death is and how we can examine it and, as the ancients did, enter it through meditation and ideas similar to the shaman's trance.

So when man related his soul to the air and as being immortal, he also saw it as partaking of the afterworld of dreams. In the Bardo Thodol (*Tibetan Book of the Dead*) there is a stage where all images are described as dream-like. The intermediary time between meeting Kali at death and then once more entering her as the womb-door is a time to see dreams, and experience the past life – and most hopefully to realize and not to be reincarnated again.

The after-world though is a place of that initial darkness of which I spoke at the beginning and again when we saw the image of Kali. It is represented, to the greater amount of the religious at least, as a dark place. The images which swell up before the mind's eye is one of darkness, and to some degree despair. For despair goes with darkness, as darkness is the unknown, and man's nature is to know. The modern archetype of the Underworld is that of the Christian Hell. Here we have the paragon of despair, pain and darkness. The flames lick the souls of the dead who are in eternal torture and damnation. The Greek Hades also has, as a part of its Underworld, the image of the pit of Tartarus. This is the place where the evil go and also those who have offended the Great God Zeus. On the whole, the Underworld of Hades is seen as a gloomy place, darkness. The Norse have their image of Nifelhiem, the lowest world on the tree Yggdrasil. This is ruled by the evil God Loki's daughter Hel. She is half alive and half dead and presents an image of despair. The Druidic belief contains the abyss Cythraul. The Hebraic Hell is Sheol and is seen as a great pit or walled city, a land of forgetfulness. The dead there live in a world of dust, darkness and covered with maggots. The Zoroastrian Hell in the far north is a place which is teeming with demons. The souls here must remain until the God Ahrimau is defeated. The Aztecs have Mictlan, ruled over by the God Mictlante-cuhtli. This hell has nine regions through which the soul must pass. The Egyptian Hell is seen as the night through which the solar barge must pass, it is called Tuat.

All these Underworld images have darkness as an image. This, I would say represents the unknown to man. We also have the death areas of the North which seem to describe a place which is again unknown to man and related to darkness. The West is also sometimes seen as the area for the dying, this is usually associated with a kinder realm, as this is the place of the sunset, a place which symbolises the death of the day. The Otherworld also is a place where the dead go and is usually seen as a lighter place, a place of permanent abode once the wheel of rebirth has been broken. The wheel of rebirth must firstly be broken though, this is done through initiatory themes such as bridges or a choice of paths which the dead soul must make.

These tests can be clearly seen again in most cultures. The Norse had this in the form of the thrice-flaming bridge Bifrost. This connected Midgard, the world of man to Asgard, the world of the Gods – a heaven or Otherworld in the sky. The Egyptian myths have the scales in the Hall of the Goddess Maat. Here the heart of the dead man is weighed against Maat's feather. If the soul has been lucky then it is taken by Horus, if unlucky, then by the triform (crocodile-hippopotamus-lion) God Amemet. Their image of hell as night also contains twelve gates, seen as the hours of the night through which the souls must pass. Each gate has guardians and tests of various kinds, if the soul is successful then it will go to the Otherworld. The Zoroastrians have the bridge Cinvato Paratu called the 'bridge of the separation'. The souls must pass this, if they are unlucky then the evil demon Vizarsh grabs them. Likewise, the Moslems believe in the bridge Sirat. The just keep their balance whilst the unjust slip to the Underworld.

The Aztec Underworld has nine hells which are tests for the soul. The soul which succeeds through all these will not be reborn but has the eternal grace of the Otherworld at his disposal. The Tibetan God of the Dead Dharma-Raja or Yama-Raja has a sword (of discrimination) in one hand and the mirror of karma in the other. The good and evil deeds of the soul are reflected in the mirror as black and white pebbles.

After this the soul is sent down one of six Lokas to be reborn as his deeds have allowed.

These initiatory tests give the soul something against which to fight, all hope is not lost after death. The Underworld should therefore be seen in most cases as a testing ground, all souls seem to go there before they ascend to heaven. It is funny when looking upon the whole spectrum of Underworlds and the dead to find the Underworld not only as a place of darkness and torture but as a place of rest for the soul in-between incarnations and a place for redemption. The Underworld can therefore be seen as not as hostile a place as one first sees it.

The Otherworld is often seen to be connected to the Underworld, or at least as the place of departure for the soul to the Otherworld. We see the loved and beautiful God Balder of the Norse myths in the Underworld. He is a God yet he too must have his time in the land of the dead. The Greek Elysium is seen as starting as one of three paths in the Underworld of Hades. The soul which has been good gradually awakens to the light and ascends through the progression of time to the higher planes. The planes of Elysium are seen to be a fertile land with many crops in a year. The Aztec Otherworld consists of three layers. The first heaven was Tlalocan which was for the flesh-soul beings which had not attained a full liberation. I suppose they might have to have been reincarnated. It is a fertile land of simple fun and games. The second heaven is Tlillan-Tlapallan, this is for the followers in life of the God Quetzalcoatl, the God-King symbolizing rebirth. This is the land of the fleshless, 'for those who had learned to live without their bodies'. This brings to mind that those who could use trance and imaginative meditation reaped the rewards by being placed in a higher heaven. The third heaven, and the highest, was Tonatiuhichan. This was 'The House of the Sun'. This heaven represented those who were fully liberated. The Druids too had a split heaven. They saw an astral plane called Gwynvyd which was close to the earth and therefore rebirth and a second called Ceugant.This second was of the soul and represented the fully illuminated being.

Other Otherworld images which man presented had varying degrees of difference. The Norse warrior heaven was that which was run by Odin. This was his hall Valhalla. The warriors rose one day, fought in battle, died and were resurrected. At night they feasted in the hall, drinking and telling tales of battle. The Vedic Tradition saw a region of light in the outer sky ruled by Yama. This was a place free of pain or misery. The Hindu saw the Otherworld as a region above the clouds. The North American Indians saw their Otherworld as the sunset in the west. This was the Happy Hunting Grounds and the land of the ancestors. The Eskimo saw their Land of the Otherworld as the Aurora Borealis, the Northern Lights. The Celt saw Avalon, the Isle of Apples as his home after proper life. The Muslim had an Otherworld which consisted of gardens in which the men resided and took their fill of women. The women then turned back into virgins.

As we have seen from the above the dead had many places to go and many things to do when they got there. The theme of judgement and initiation was common. This started in life as living 'properly' and later after death as the ordeals to be overcome. Man saw death not only as the point of death in the image of the Death Goddess and Death God but also as a happy land at times. The light though was behind the darkness, just like the way in which we must look behind the image of Kali, the Death aspect of the Goddess, to see the treasures of the Otherworld or rebirth. Too often man does not see further than his own nose. To see into the image of death we must look at the projections of man's imagination and delve into the reality of the situation. Man must know death, because, as we explained before, he must not have uncertainties in his equation of life.

To overcome the uncertainty man must meditate and fully come to realise the image of death. This is done not only through meditation on such figures as Kali, but through initiation. This is the start of the road to religion, and is the start to the road to knowing one's own death. As we shall see in the next chapters, man uses death in many ways and experiences it in many ways. All these are to give the human being an understanding of life after death, light after darkness.

EXPERIENCING DEATH

"But the point is that if you can fantasise the idea of being nothing for always and always, what you are really saying is after I'm dead the universe stops, and what I'm saying is it goes on just as it did when you were born."

– Alan Watts, *Death*

"Whatever is here, that is there; what is there, the same is here. He who seeth here as different, meeteth death after death. By mind alone this is to be realised, and (then) there is no difference here. From death to death he goeth, who seeth as if there is a difference here."

– Dr. W.Y. Evans-Wentz, *Katha Upanishad*

Death is, in a physical sense, a slow process which takes time to become complete. Some would argue that it is perhaps never complete. The body, after what we call death (the physical cesation of pulse and brain activity), continues for some time to live; the hair grows and certain cellular functions continue. The body is still in an organised mass and is therefore an entity with structure and life. Only when it has completely dissolved and has no more living and structuring components is it seen to be dead. Lyall Watson shows in his book *The Romeo Error* that there is in fact no particular time of biological death. He is a biologist and will therefore see things in this manner.

We, on the esoteric trail of death, see the time of death as the time when the vital spirit leaves the body. The spirit being the energy and dynamism behind life as a force which is necessary for complete functioning on all planes. When it is changed (as energy can never be destroyed) the conciousness of that energy (seen as the soul in this case) moves onward to that plane. The soul and spirit are inseperable and are in fact a part of one another, in some senses the same.

The soul however, as consciousness of spirit, can leave the body. Yogins from the East have gone into a temporary hibernation for weeks, and in some cases months, leaving outsiders wondering whether they are alive or dead. In meditation too, on higher levels, the soul can leave the body and experience things which are of a different nature altogether. When shamans do this they are seen to be dead, or at least temporarily dead. When we dream it is sometimes thought that the soul wanders in vacation of the physical body, this too can be seen as a little or temporary death. The Aborigines make much of dreams and the vacation of the soul. A brilliant modern example of this can be found in the Australian film *The Last Wave* which deals with such matters in a dreamlike manner. Sickness too is seen as a vacation of the soul, or a wandering soul.

The belief in this little death, or in other words the vacation of the soul from the body, is the prime requisite for travel and experience of death and its worlds. It was this technique which must be mastered for man to know death and to have a spiritual vocation 'proper'.

Barbara Walker says "Men have usually believed that knowledge of death can only come from those who have experienced it". This all goes to show that the sacred men and women of religion and ecstasy belief systems such as shamanism must have experience of death. This came about at initiation which is the death and rebirth of the initiate.

Initiation is common to all religions in some form or another. It may have become merely symbolic but the truth is that one must have an understanding of that niggling uncertainty – death. Man must have knowledge of it, especially when he is in a spiritual capacity. How can he teach it if he himself has not experienced it? That is what the elaborate initiations were for, to give the initiate an experience of death and to teach him techniques which aided the same effect.

The Norse initiation is said (by Michael Howard) to have taken place in nine caves. These caves represented the nine Underworld Kingdoms of the Norse tree of life, Yggdrasil. In the various rooms the initiate would presumably have spent a night. The final cave was the final realisation; Howard says that in this last cave was placed a mirror into which the initiate looked. The old occult axiom 'Man, Know Thyself' is here reflected. Man looked into the mirror and saw that he must look within to find both his death and knowledge. Odin, top of the Norse mythological system, is said to have hung upon a bough of the Yggdrasil for nine nights to gain wisdom of the runes. This is his descent into the nine worlds of the Underworld in search of knowledge – in effect an initiation.

"I know that I hung
on the windswept tree
for nine full nights,
wounded by a spear
and given to Odin,
myself to myself;
on that tree
of which none know
from what roots it rises."

So said Odin. His initiation was much more, it was a God sacrificing to a God. His initiation in connection to the tree also shows us the ancient shamanic forms of initiation which usually involved a tree climbing ritual. The tree was the centre of the worlds and from it the soul could venture either to the Underworld or above to the Gods in the Otherworld.

So we can see so far that initiation is related to death in that the soul must leave the body – this in itself is a small death. The soul must also venture to the Underworld via the tree of wisdom to gain knowledge, in particular of the dead. Initiation also often took place in the dark or in solitude. When a shaman was chosen through dream he often went mad, to be found days later raving at the top of a tree. Often the shaman would just go into the wilderness for a time of solitude in which to contemplate and contact the dead. It was of vital importance that the would-be spiritual man or woman seek out solitude and enter within themselves. They would have to die and be reborn as the new shaman or spiritual person. The Ammasalik Eskimos who are up for initiation into the shamanic society are told to find an area of solitude and there to rub two stones together. The rubbing of stones may last all through the summer. Finally though the initiate will have a vision in which he is stripped of flesh (killed) and then resurrected. In Labrador the Eskimo's Great Spirit comes and devours the candidate. As Eliade shows, also in Greenland, the spirit appears and devours the candidate and he is dead for three days.

Along with this death and resurrection are visualisations and meditations, to which we shall return in the next chapter. These are designed to enable the aspirant to die and be reborn again mentally. In short to know his own death and through that all death. The initiate is often seen to have been pulled apart and his brain or entrails washed and placed back again. His body is also often named bone by bone in a secret language. This process gives him a new body and a new being in which he can become a sacred man/woman. It is also a point which we should make clear that the soul is often seen to reside in the bones of the living being. Thus when the shaman contemplates his bones he contemplates his soul, the renaming of the bones also indicates a new being with knowledge. Eliade says; "But in all these cases reduction to the skeleton indicates a passing beyond the profane human condition and, hence, a deliverance from it."

The bones of animals in these soul-bone societies were not broken but must be ritually treated, either by burial or throwing them into the sea. The Norse God Thor had the power to bring back to life the animal from the dead just by wrapping the bones in the hide and hitting it with his hammer Mjollnir. In one instance he was angered because someone, whilst eating the goat, had broken a leg to eat the marrow. When Thor revived the goat it limped, its soul had in effect been damaged!

The death experience of the initiation would be the first of many death experiences for the spiritually minded. Later in such societies as the shamanic, the death was again enacted. In the trance the magician was seen to die. The normal layout of a trance session started with a rythmic beating of a drum, the actor would then dance and exhaust himself to the point of passing out. Once this stage had been reached he would go into a deep meditation in which his body was totally still. This was seen, by those surrounding the actor, as being dead. All present thought that he had died and his soul had gone upon the tree to travel to the Otherworld. The shaman or actor would use various techniques which Eliade calls 'ecstatic' to release the soul from the body. These were induced, as mentioned before, by dancing, by drugs, by concentrative meditation etc. They all have the element of excitation within them; whether that be physically or mentally. The body and mind reach a pitch at which the soul is released, the body is then seen to be dead, as in common sleep. The purpose for this departure and death experience is usually seen to be for the benefit of the tribe. It could be to discover whether some taboo had been broken and hence the run of bad hunting the tribe had been experiencing. Prophecy too was common in these trances and also healing the sick. As mentioned before it was a pagan view that the sick were such because the soul had left the body. It was therefore the duty of those who knew the geography of the death-worlds to restore the soul.

The main function of the shaman was then to go to the realms of death and instruct the people of its geography. The death of a person was a time in particular when the shaman was needed, it was a time to help the dead by giving them instruction on how to get to the Underworld. If this was not carried out correctly the soul would return and haunt the tribe. The shaman therefore either had to go with and direct the soul or describe in pictographical manner the geography the soul passed through. Other rites were often used to ensure that the soul arrived at its otherworldly destination and did not return.

This description and explanation of the after-life geography is common not only to the shamanic peoples but also to the Tibetan and the Egyptian. *The Bardo Thodol* was a book to be studied by the living, it was said that to understand it and live it were to live a better life. *The Bardo Thodol* or *Tibetan Book of the Dead* has come under much study, we shall just note here that it was a guide to the intermediary time of forty-nine days (7x7) between death and rebirth into a womb. In Dr. C.G. Jung's words; "The text falls into three parts. The first part, called the *Chikhai Bardo*, describes the psychic happenings at the moment of death. The second part, or *Chonyid Bardo* deals with the dream-state which supervenes immediately after death, and with what are called 'karmic illusions'. The third part, or *Sidpa Bardo*, concerns the onset of the birth-instinct and of prenatal events".

So here we see that man, when obtaining the ability to read could himself become educated in the after-death state. The trance-shaman was no longer needed. These guides precluded the modern manuals which have upsurged from the interest they first brought about at the beginning of this century. Likewise these new manuals gave prayers and insights into the world beyond and between life. Timothy Leary, the prophet of L.S.D., was the first and the foremost to proclaim the use of psychedelics in combination with the *Bardo Thodol.* His poetic book, *Pyschedelic Experience*, was based upon the *Bardo Thodol* and was divided into similar chapters which corresponded to the death, dream and rebirth states of the *Bardo Thodol.* In conjunction with the hallucigenic drug L.S.D., these were to be read and related to the 'high' obtained. The experiences were to be akin to experiences in actuality after death; some of them, especially the illusions of the demons, could be quite frightening. What we gain from these however is that man was once again trying to penetrate the veil of the unknown and prepare himself as best he could for his eventual demise.

The use of drugs is used to bypass the use of meditation and trance-ecstasy techniques. Although the shaman too used drugs he did not use them as a total means of technique, but rather as a compliment. The L.S.D of Leary was edging away from technique into the realms of instant death and rebirth. Yet, what man gains from these experiences, whether real or illusionary, is a power over death. These people are the makers of death through their experiences, they give life and form to the otherwise unknown. All of the common men must rely totally upon their dreams and what this man says about the death-world, unless of course they too enter ecstatic technique or the use of drugs.

The use of drugs is common to both ancient and modern man as a means of releasing the soul. The modern one is the above-mentioned L.S.D. Huxley, upon his deathbed, had his wife inject him with a small dose of the drug to help him assimilate to the experience; for, above all, death must be enjoyed. It is a belief that the state of your mind when you die will reflect how the intermediary states act. Similar to the above are experiments which have been going on both in the U.S.A. and here in England with L.S.D. and the dying. Most people in hospital die with so many drugs in them that the reality of the situation is not apparent. With L.S.D. the patient is able to live through and realize the death experience. They are therefore no longer afraid of what was unknown but rather look forward to it in a relaxed state of mind.

Castaneda, the American shaman, trained by a Yaqui Indian shaman, used drugs as a large part of his training. Frequently he comments on a separate reality and also on the death-like effect of the drugs; he was often immobilized by some of the drugs to the extent of appearing dead. He was not particularly involved with the death aspect but we can surmise that the death-like posture he took in the use of these drugs is not unlike the common small-death exhibited by other death-orientated peoples. Indeed, Don Juan, his teacher, said that every Man of Knowledge must know his own death and that it should sit beside him on his mat! This surely shows that under the drug orientated systems like the above we also find death as the unknown and hidden aspect of the equation. Death in any system such as this is that which must be realized if one is to suceed and gain final liberation. It can best be perceived as the ultimate and initial initiation which must 'take' properly, for faking will do no one any accord, but rather bring death as the wretched hag which it is to the unkowing.

Eliade says; "We must also take into consideration the symbolic value of narcotic intoxication. It was equivalent to a 'death'; the intoxicated person left his body, acquired the condition of ghosts and spirits". This is in relation to the shamanic trance, although narcotics of various kinds were used it was seen as a degradation from original technique to do so. As is common among the shamanic peoples, it was seen that there was once a time when technique and contact with the other worlds was easy and could be accomplished by anyone. The use of drugs and the death experience, especially during initiation is extremely common. Islamic mystics made use of hashish; in the Jivaro training, along with being beaten uncounscious, the initiate was forced to fast and only drink tobacco juice; the North and South American Indians used Jimson Weed to gain visions of spirits; and we even know that Patanjali in his Yoga-Sutras says that medicinal plants (ausadhi) can be used as an aid or supplement to samadhi.

The death state which the drugs exhibited was likened to the experiencing of death in that the taker was seen to leave his body and 'fly' to the otherworlds. Castaneda gives a detailed account of his attempting to change into a bird and fly when in a drugged stupor. The bird is often related to the magical flight and the release of the soul to the realm of the dead. As we saw before Lleu took the form of an eagle when killed by Gronw. Likewise the shamans often relate to their costume as a bird's wings or skeleton. This seems to have some implications of an exterior soul, and hence a strong relation to the dead.

Seeing spirits too had a content of experiencing death. "For in this manner, having contact with the souls of the dead signifies being dead oneself." Thus in dreams man saw that he had acquired the body of the dead and had experienced death, albeit in a small way. This was seen to have been a spiritual condition. Much reliance was placed upon dreams and there interpretation. Often people went into the jungle, wood or wilderness in order to obtain a vision or dream of symbolic form. This was seen as coming from the dead, the dead were relied upon heavily and seen to be 'those with knowledge'. Nikolai Tolstoy remarks in his book *The Quest for Merlin*; "The details follow a pattern familiar from Celtic and Norse literature, in which, significantly, such dreams were in early times frequently induced in special incubation chambers attached to temples". Often churches or holy places would have these incubation rooms in which the seeker would specifically search for a significant dream in relation to their question. I suppose it is a form of prophesy by the dead! Other means of inducing such states were to sleep in strange surroundings. Of course, the strangest were grave-yards and burial grounds in which contact with the dead was close at hand and almost assured. It was said that all who slept on a fairy hill or burial mound would either be dead, mad or a poet in the morning.

As we saw earlier with relation to the Eskimo (Inuit), they are told to search out isolation and there to seek a vision, this is to be connected with the dead. It often appears in myth that people go out and later come back from isolation, though upon their return they are much changed. This is seen as journeying and experiencing death. Jesus in the Christian myth goes into the wilderness for forty days. Here he is tempted etc., what we see is that he was isolated and went to the realm of the dead; the dead being signified by the devil as Christian ruler of the Underworld. The dead are those who know, therefore one seeks out communion with the dead in order to know.

Prophecy by the dead is common but it strays a little from our theme as it is not the experience of death but rather prophesy from. Dream however is a direct experience in relation to death as it is seen to be in the death world that the soul of the dreamer travels. Prophecy from bones and entrails is common. The Yukagir use skulls of their ancestors, preferably those of shamans or wise men. Tibetan Lamas have skull drums and trumpets made of human bone. The drum stick too is of the human. Casting lots can also be seen to have a link with bones of the dead. The most interesting similarity between the bones and the dead is the shaman's costume. This contains iron decorations said to resemble human bones; the shaman also often prophecies, always within his costume. Bones were also used in divination by throwing them onto a fire and watching where cracks appeared. Whichever direction the crack appeared the tribe would hunt.

The OOBE (out-of-body-experiences) are also a modern connection with the experience of death. These often occur when the person involved has some traumatic experience such as an operation or road crash. The person leaves the body in astral form and watches what is happening around his body. These are most common in the death sense when someone actually dies on the operating table and is then revived. Documentation of this is vast and it shows that the soul is released from the body upon the ceasing of the heartbeat. The experiences gained are various but usually comfortable and relaxed; even on occasion an unwillingness to return to the living. There are never any conceptions of the state of torture and flames which the Christians try and bring across. The whole OOBE is a fascinating area of research but often the reliance is upon astral and not actual soul-death travel experience.

Other experiences of death as the actual process have been recorded. These are usually in connection with accidents in which death as a thought is inevitable. Lyall Watson, in his research for *The Romeo Error* came across the writings of a man called Albert Heim. He was a mountaineer and had a near-death experience when he fell whilst climbing. He later collated other experiences of climbing accidents. What emerged were four distinct stages; the first was the reflex action of attempting to prevent the inevitable; secondly there were unassociated thoughts dealing with minor day-to-day events of no consequence; thirdly there was a past life review in which the main events of life are seen; lastly there was a mystical experience similar to ecstasy in which the person concerned is in a state of rapture. These stages show that the inevitable death promotes a defence against pain and the thought of death. The last stage resembles that which preceeds the shamanic ecstatic magical flight. Ecstasy is seen as the experience of the soul and things in connection with it. Mystical states of consequence are said to start with rapture and uninvolvement of that which surrounds the self.

There seems to be another death-instinct experience which comes on in danger. This can be related to death-feigning when the best posture for Survival is one in which the attacker thinks the victim is dead. There is a lot to be said about this. When living in Canada we were told that if attacked by a Grizzly or Brown bear whilst hiking, it was best to feign death. This would prevent the bear from continuing the attack and thus increase survival chance. Insects and animals also have this death-experience. When in danger of attack or in the process of being attacked they pretend to be dead. Scientific studies show that in fact the animal is wide awake and alert. Another interesting thing is that the animal takes up a position which it thinks to be the correct posture of death. This posture is not the natural death posture but rather the one the attacked expects the attacker to expect.

So, not only does man experience death in mystical states but also when under threat of attack. In some shamanic tribes the inititate is scared out of his wits or beaten unconscious; presumably to take the death and protective posture and relive death.

The experience of death is something which is wide-spread. As we saw, it is best and most commonly seen in connection with initiation where the initiate is seen to die and then to be resurrected from the dead. The newly initiated member is then seen to be a new person usually with new magical powers. It is the process of dying however, which is of consequence. One must have a knowledge of the death and dream-world if one is to make contact with it. As the religious world is made up of Gods and the souls of the dead then it is presumed that to be in contact with this is the way of power and knowledge. Initiation also often starts with the seeker being told to enter the wilderness of the unknown and there to search out spirit guides, visions, dreams or dead ancestors. These are the connection with the otherworlds and the dead which are necessary to initiation. The initiate therefore does not necessarily have to die and be reborn but rather has to have an experience of the death world.

As we also saw there are divine figures which describe this descent into the Underworld in order to gain knowledge: Jesus and the Devil, and Odin and the nine Underworld levels of the Norse tree Yggdrasil. The tree is also related to the death world in that, that which is above and below are worlds of things not alive. The seeker for knowledge must therefore enter these worlds, either through initiation, dreams or meditation. The Cross of Christianity is in effect a World Tree. Likewise the Mount Meru of the *Bardo Thodol* is the way to the divine light (Dharma-Kaya). The modern system being used by the Western Mystery Tradition is also linked with the tree symbolism. This is, of course, the Cabalistic Tree of Life. The symbolism of this tree represents all in man's mind and that above in the realms of the Gods. There is also a Nightside to the tree which represents the darker forces of each sphere (Sephira), these can be equated to the Underworld kingdoms of the tree.

The experience which the seeker gains from his initial experience will go to the future in that it aids his following attempts at journeying amongst the dead. This is indeed an archaic technique and grew with man's first magical system, that of shamanism The trance of the shaman and to some extent the samadhi of the yogi are alike. They both incorporate concentrative techniques which enable them to delve into the death world beyond the living body. Some yogis have taken the techniques so far that their bodies may be buried for days on end without any apparent physical demise.

The whole realm of the spiritual is tied up with the idea of death and its experience. The ancient holy men covered their bodies with ash of the earth, for death was their destiny. Anything in a spiritual concept which touched the fringes of the otherworld beings was death related. But, like we saw in the first chapter, death is not the forbidding wretch which we at first see in the face of Kali Ma. The experience of death has its own rewards. As we shall see in the next chapter, meditating on death and in particular, one's own death, have great spiritual and pyschological implications.

DEATH MEDITATION

"You get this sense of nothingness, just like you've got the sense of nothing behind your eyes, very powerful frisky nothingness underlying your whole being. There's nothing in that nothing to be afraid of. With that sense you can come on like the rest of your life is gravy because you're already dead: You know you're going to die."
— Alan Watts in *Death*.

"All that we are is the result of what we have thought: it is founded on our thoughts, it is made up of our thoughts." — Dhammapada.

"This room an antechamber is:
Beyond the Hall of Very Bliss!
Quick, Death! for underneath thy door
I see the glimmering of Heaven's floor."
—Huw Morus from *A Celtic Anthology* by Grace Rhys.

"To reach the ceilings of Heaven – look within."
— Austin Osman Spare.

The meditation of death, dying and beyond is not what most of modern man would think to be a healthy occupation. In fact, it would probably be seen as a touch morbid. However, the meditation of one's own death in particular was, and is, a fact of initiation. To realise one's own death is to banish forever any uncertainties of the future.

Tom Chetwynd, in his *A Dictionary of Symbols* says this of death and its experience; "Symbolic Death/Actual Death: We cannot experience, or anyway savour the moment of actual death. As with our own bodies we can only experience death through the imagination. The value of the experience appears to be that it leads to individual wholeness." It is by meditation and imagination (now called path-working that the individual attains this state of wholeness, having experienced death,

29

in his mind. Whether this can be seen to be a real death experience is debatable, as is the use of drugs, visions, dreams etc. In fact the whole feild of death-experience is debatable. Whether the man who fell off the mountaintain really had a death experience is hard to say; some say that it is a defence mechanism within the mind to prevent the thought of extinction. Whether, again, the man who dies on the operating table has really experienced death is also debatable. These experiences are so personal that only those who experience them can attest their validity. What man can do is search out the death experience through meditation or trance and decide for themselves. I for one, having been a concentrative meditator for three years, can attest that the soul is real and that the body can only be seen to be its temporary home.

The other question which arises is whether or not the mind is causing such projections of what it estimates death will be like. This is a viable proposition in that people's experiences of the after-life plane of death are usually what they conceive them to be. This however, does not mean that they are false. Man is commonly seen to be his own God, especially in the Aquarian Age. This is not a new view but one which has always existed. The ancient pagans saw their ancestors turn into Gods through the progression of time. Figures such as Jesus, Odin, King Arthur, Merlin etc., are said perhaps to have once existed. The shamanic sprits were often seen as ancestors, guiding their relatives through the death-world. I for one, say that man creates his after-death world with his own mind. It is he who creates and experiences it. The *Bardo Thodol* gives the impression that one should have the correct thoughts at the time of death. Wentz quotes Sri Krishna talking to Arjuna in the *Bhagavad Gita* as saying; "One attaineth whatever state (of being) one thinketh about at the last when relinquishing the body, being ever absorbed in the thought thereof".

The thought of creating one's own after-life, and perhaps subsequent rebirth, are not uncommon. The initiate is often instructed as to what he should see in the imaginative meditations and how he should interpret them. The only degree of spontaneity I can find is where the shaman-to-be goes out after a dream and enters the wilderness of death. He was not instructed as to what to experience yet all the same experienced the death world and its spirits. We also find, as mentioned before; that in the OOBEs there were no conceptions of the Christian Hell. However, at the other end of the spectrum we find those who have been indoctrinated with such aids as mandalas. The *Bardo Thodol* was often read in life and mantras and mandalas were used in conjunction with its contemplation.

However the meditation of the bones and the strippng away of the flesh appears to be very old indeed. Eliade says; "We incline to believe that this type of meditation belongs to an archaic, pre-Buddhistic, stratum of spirituality, which was based, in one way or another, on the ideology of the hunting peoples and whose object was to 'withdraw' the soul from the practitioner's own body for a mystical journey – that is, to achieve ecstasy". Ecstasy and its techniques are certainly old. And the methods employed in meditation and the like are designed to give ecstasy and thus a release of the soul; and this is related to the death-experience. The initiate was often told, as we mentioned before, to search out solitude. Some rites, as the Tibetan chod rite demonstrates, took place in graveyards. The Trappist monks of Mount St. Bernard in Leicestershire do likewise, they meditate in graveyards about eternity.

Let us now examine some of the death-meditation rites of which this book is about.

The Tibetan tantric rite called chod demonstrates this very clearly. The rite takes place to the sound of a drum (made of a human skull) and a trumpet (made from a human thighbone). This rite uses the force of meditation to imagine the demons devouring one's own flesh and blood. In a way the meditator is sacrificing himself as did Odin and Jesus. The rite continues with a visualisation. The music and dancing which initiate the rite are used to attract the spirits for the rather sinister meal. Meanwhile the meditator sees the death aspect of the Goddess, something along the lines of Kali, approach him with a sword. With this she decapitates and cuts him to pieces; ". . .then the demons and wild beasts rush on the still quivering fragments, eat the flesh, and drink the blood". The process goes on to describe how the Buddha offered his own flesh to starving animals and man-eating demons. Eliade thinks though that this later addition was "Buddhist coloring", and the initial rite was ancient.

We saw earlier how the Ammasalik Eskimo shaman told his protege to seek out solitude and there to rub two stones together. This sacred solitude is to be beside an old grave or by a lake. The bear of the lake is then to appear and eat all the initiate's flesh, leaving him with just a skeleton. When the vision is over he is told that his flesh and clothes will rush to him and re-clothe him in his mortal garment. Also in the shape of a bear is the Great Spirit Tongarsoak, this devours the Eskimo of Labrador. In relation to the Eskimo Eliade again says; "Success in obtaining this experience requires his making a long effort of physical privation and mental contemplation directed to gaining the ability to see himself as a skeleton". As we already know, the bones are seen as the soul and therefore the immortal part of the initiate. By stripping away the flesh and having only the bones left he has, in effect, become of the dead and immortal. His transient and mortal flesh no longer matter. The Eskimo also has to name each bone in turn. This whole procedure is that of death-experience as initiation and consecration of the self by renaming.

The Siberian shaman does not use the same concentrative meditation technique which appears to be the most common. Instead it occurs in a dream and indicates that he has become a shaman, whether he wished it or not. The same practice occurs; the images of Gods and spirits rip the flesh from his body and then re-name each bone in turn. Again, this is the consecration and initiation. It has been seen that to strip away the flesh and make oneself is to re-enter ". . .the womb of this primordial life, that is, to a complete renewal, a mystical rebirth".

In Indo-Tibetan tantrism the yogin again has the same technique as that of the Eskimo; that is he must, by mind alone, strip away the flesh and present the skeleton to the light of day. The initiate is told to imagine or visualize his body as a corpse and his head as the death aspect of the Goddess. His head, as Goddess, is to be seen holding a knife and a skull. The Goddess then cuts the head from the corpse and proceeds to chop the yogin's body into tiny pieces; these are then thrown to the devouring dieties who eat them. This visualization has the common aspect of self sacrifice. One is, in a manner, taking part of the divine, because one is, in a sense, being eaten and destroyed by the divine. This type of meditation also goes to show a self-creation, only those who try will know of its efficacy.

Another meditation consists of the meditator seeing himself as a pure white skeleton which issues flames, so large are the flames that they "fill the voidness of the Universe". Yet another tells the meditator to see himself as the angry Goddess Dakini. As the Goddess he strips the flesh off of his own corpse; "Visualize thyself as .... that thou .... spreadest it (the skin) out so that it covereth the Third-Void Universe, and upon it heapest up all thy bones and flesh. Then, when the malignant spirits are in the midst of enjoying the feast, imagine that the Wrathful Dakini taketh the hide and rolleth it up .... and dasheth it down forcibly, reducing it and all its contents to a mass of bony and fleshy pulp, upon which many mentally-produced beasts feed".

The above is an interesting extract from what would have been a complete and long meditation. The instruction would have been simple, the actual process of imagining them would have been long. The whole process was to have been gone through very clearly in the meditator's own mind. Not however only as mind, but rather as the soul released through ecstatic meditation. The ripping of the flesh was to be felt as pain, the devouring demons to arouse hate and fear, and finally to realize utter destruction. The meditator, once again in the wake-world, would have an experience which would last forever.

Zen and the Sufi mysticism also have the idea of extinguishing themselves in order to cross the death threshold. Other eastern schools of thought produced meditations which ended with the dissolution of the 'I' into no perception. This state of meditation was beyond the common object-subject of yoga and was a state which was not perceivable; it was in effect a state of 'No-Being' or 'No-Thing'. This was seen as the ultimate realization, that man was in fact a mere illusion, and that the course of our spiritual lives was to realize that we were in fact nothing at all.

The most common experiences of the death-meditation are those experienced in trance by the shaman. These are in fact meditations and are accompanied by the common meditational aids; rhythmic drumming, chanting, concentration and on occasion, drugs. Often, while in trance, a reader would relay the geography through which the shaman passed, making the meditation a descriptive pathworking. Among the Ostyak shamans the trance was undertaken in sleep after eating either three or seven mushrooms of one of the toxic varieties. The use of drugs was however seen to be valid; "It was equivalent to a 'death'; the intoxicated person left his body, and acquired a condition of ghosts and spirits. Mystical ecstasy being assimilated to a temporary 'death' or to leaving the body".

Above all else, the meditation should take on the form of a 'death' where the soul, as the 'great experiencer', left and saw the death-world and had experience of the same.

The greatest example we can give for the Tibetan and modern death meditation is perhaps that which accompanies the *Bardo Thodol.* We have seen how initiation is accompanied with death meditation yet the use of this book is not a 'great' initiation but rather an every day occurance. In conjunction with reading the book, the meditator would gaze upon mandalas, or pictures of the various stages of the after-death state. The intermediary state of dreams was seen as a time in which good and evil demons and spirits visited the deceased. There were also temptations of sex and worldly pleasures. These were to be avoided. The mandalas accustomed the meditator to what he was to see, he would therefore know how to interpret the karmic visions and to seize the opportunity to gain the divine light. Also there is the fact that there are some, presumably those with knowledge of the after death state, who can choose the womb and life into which they will be reincarnated. The meditation of the death pattern is therefore an attempt by mortal man to see behind the veil and to accustom himself to what will one day become a reality.

Death meditation therefore serves, not only as an initiatory sequence in which to gain a new body, but also a means to prepare for death. As we said before, it is those with knowledge of death, and hence the unknown, who command respect and high religious station. It can be seen that death meditation is a part of any mystery cult and in some regions of the world it is much more; it is a part of life, and a necessary part at that.

The death meditation can now be seen to fill a large number of purposes. It is also used in various ways and the most common and best documented is that of the shamanic trance and any other trance throughout history. Trance is a large part of religious and magical structure. In such magical societies, one has no power unless the trance comes freely; that is unless one can perform as a guide in the death world. The religious also must have this knowledge, for they are the people who bury the dead. This, however, was not always the case, and in some societies the shaman would bury the dead and carry out the funerary rites. The reason for this was that the religious structure of the area did not have people who were well versed in the after-life geography, or who could enter a death meditation.

The Nightmare is also closely linked with these meditations and dreams in which the shaman or prophet is visited. The Goddess, as we saw in the first chapter, can be seen to be tri-form; the last section is that of the death Goddess or, as she is often called, the Nightmare. Her relation to these meditations is common, as we saw above. The reason for this is that man, as we saw earlier, saw her as the picture of death. Having her in the meditations was therefore a prime figure of the change which death brings. The meditations hosted the worst that can be; the tearing apart of the limbs; the ripping of the flesh and the cooking of the bones; the devouring of the skin, blood and flesh; and finally the pulping and smashing of all that is of oneself. This whole process gives the meditator a power over the death of pain and rather lets him realize that there is nothing worse than his own memory and mind. It is also common in history for people who are in extreme pain from disease (and hence the Goddess) to become enlightened. The whole idea of nightmares and pain give rise to enlightenment. Certainly in some meditation systems one is told that instead of ignoring a twitching or a cramped pain, instead to concentrate upon it and transcend it. The transcending of pain can bring ecstasy, and above all else the death realization; we automatically associate death with pain. Francis Huxley quotes an Eskimo shaman: "All wisdom is found far from men, in the great solitude, and it can be acquired only through suffering. Privations and suffering are the only things that can open a man's mind to that which is hidden". This again shows the association between pain, suffering and isolation which are to bring man the release or vision which he is searching for. He then goes on to comment on the aspect which was the attacker or danger in the meditation or vision: "What happens then is that the attacker – be it human, animal, spirit or disease – is turned into a helper, because it has been suffered, overcome, and made obedient". We again see here that which I talked about in relation to the Goddess as Kali. Once the darkness has been overcome (the greatest darkness being the unknown – death) it ceases to be a pain and becomes, instead, a helper and a light. Thus the man or woman who has gone through a death meditation experience in all its intensity, or a similar dream-nightmare, will have power over death and thus have its knowledge as an aid.

We can now clearly see what function death meditation took and how it was envisaged. The examples I gave before were ones which described the stripping of the flesh to the skeleton, because this is the way man views his own death. Yet death meditations can be as simple as the Trappist Monks and their contemplation of eternity in a graveyard; or perhaps the mental visualization of a partirular aspect of the Goddess as death. On the other hand one may choose to view death as nothing and therefore enter into it, diminishing (by the power of the mind) himself to nothing. All these and many more are death meditations, one does not necessarily have to see one's own self devoured; that is more in the initiatory line. If one wishes one can just experience death in an outer form as the Goddess or eternity. However, to truly know the death realms and the power to control that uncertainty, then you will surely have to experience the death of the self. Death therefore takes on two aspects, that of one's own self dying and that of the vision of death.

DEATH MEDITATIONS

"I come, and I AM Life. In me there is no death, for I have died and conquered death". — Anthony Duncan, *Lord of the Dance.*

Nachiketas talking to Death: *"This doubt indeed arose even to the gods, and you say, O Death, that it is difficult to understand; but no greater teacher than you can explain it, and there is no other boon so great as this".* — Katha Upanishad.

We have now seen how man sees death, how he comes to terms with and conquers it. The only way in which it can be conquered is to experience it; that is done by imitating, dreaming or meditating on death. What follows here is a short description of meditation as a simple yogic guideline, similar to that used in trance. The form I give here is that which is rendered (with slight personal moderations) from Patanjali's *Yoga-Sutras.* This concentrative technique is a means of directing the mind to any point desired and there to enter into it, in a sense, to become it. This technique has been used for hundreds of years in various forms by totally unrelated peoples. The shamanic peoples often used concentrative meditation to induce trance; the American Indian Sun Dance was a severe form of concentrative meditation, using pain as the aid of transcendency. The meditations which follow are simple, some are in the form of pathworkings; these are simply descriptive passages upon which the meditator contemplates and follows. The pathworkings are designed to get the meditator to follow certain paths leaving room for personal mind expression, experience and impression.

There are eight parts, or limbs to Patanjali's meditational system. These are designed, as a cohesive whole, to bring the meditator into not only the correct procedure, but also the correct lifestyle. We will, unfortunately, have to ignore the first two parts as these are basically designed for a monastic lifestyle suitable to purity of mind and body. They are in effect a set of rules or a moral code. These first two are called Yama and Niyama. Yama is 'forbearance' and consists of five elements; no killing, veracity, no stealing, continence and not coveting. The five Niyamas are; purification, contentment, austerity, inaudible mutterings and preserving devotion to the Lord. Obviously these would be interpreted in a different manner in the light of modern society. We all, however, have our own moral system and mannerisms which keep us at a level which we see as acceptable.

The last six are to do with meditation and that which is conclusive

Meditating on eternity in the abode of the dead in the cemetery of the English Trappists.

to its success. They are:

1. Posture/Asana: A correct and alert posture, usually with the neck and back erect to allow a clean and easy flow of breath. The posture should be such that it can be maintained for the length of the meditation/pathworking without strain.

2. Suppression of the breath/Pranayama: A regular and relaxed flow of breath which should become subconscious once controlled. It may however be controlled to such an extent that it causes the sensation of bliss, this being achieved by slowing the breath down and holding it on either the in or out breath. The strain however, when perfectly done, should last the duration of the meditation. Overstrain is not advisable.

3. Restraint/Pratyahara: The introspection of the mind. Closing the human circuit from the outside world to prepare for inner viewing.

4. Attention/Dharana: Concentration with the mind or body (usually the navel centre) upon the chosen object(s) of meditation.

5. Contemplation/Dhyana: Knowledge from the subject to object. The world, now closed off, is not seen, but rather all that is, is the subject and object and a perfect stream of information. The body etc. does not exist. This stage is often linked with ecstacy and is the lower and access state to Samadhi.

6. Meditation/Samadhi: Only the object now exists. The subject (you) are totally with the object and therefore of the object. States reach beyond this to higher states of Samadhi, it will suffice, however, to remain with this Samadhi.

As I mentioned before, there are certain aids to meditation which are incorporated into the trance techniques. These include drugs, mantra, mandala, chanting, music etc. The list goes on. Some forms of trance, like that of the shaman's contains a stage show for the audience. In this the shaman becomes excited and the crowd feeds on this, in turn giving power to the trance-worker. When exhausted from these exploits, which may include such things as energetic dancing or playing a drum, the shaman feigns death and enters the meditational state. Such preludes to meditation are common. Anything which inspires may be utilized in the hopes of transcending normal consciousness. The poet, like that of Robert Graves, may use the figure of the nine-fold muse to excite the process of inspiration and thus soul-release; at least in part. What you may do is up to you. There are many ways of approaching meditation, and when we take the death meditation we enter a very personal view of what it should be like. What I give as pathworkings can be used, yet the reliance for realization is upon you as the meditator to search out the images which are best for you.

One who is 'into' Indian art and culture may find the Kali drawing, such as the one in this book, of enormous aid; others will find it a complete blank. One may prefer to take a death-Goddess from one's own pantheon. Perhaps Cerridwen as the White Phantom or white sow would suit? Or perhaps the wretch of Black Annis? There are literally thousands of images for one to choose from. One may wish to contemplate nothingness as one's ideal of the death state – this would perhaps suit the aetheist best. Images incorporating the Tree of Life are perhaps the best and most accessible symbols of the death-world we can use. The Tree can be used as the ladder upon which descent or ascent can be made, both ways are trips to the non-human death-world. The descent though is the most common and deals with human death as the soul between incarnations. One might also like to use known geography of certain cultures; the Underworld realm of Hades for those of Greek orientation; the night land of Tuat for those of Egyptian; Nifleheim and the nine Underworld Kingdoms for those of a Norse persuasion; or for those of a pagan view, maybe a trip through the mound and spiral.

So many visions of death and its manners, we are really spoilt for choice. However, I have brought a few of the elements of death together in a small variety of death-ideas which follow.

DEATH IN THE WORLD

Imagine you are approaching an accident, just in front of you in the centre of a steep road. Two cars have collided and are upturned. The image which presents itself to you is one of slow motion, stillness; sound is blocked, all is a frame by frame happening.

You approach the wreckage slowly, cautiously, your eyes fixed upon the wreckage. What has happened you wonder. Are they alright? Are they dead? The fear and thoughts of dead bodies you see in your mind are whirling at a great pace, getting quicker as you approach. What will you see?

Reaching the wreckage you bend down and peer into the smashed and bloodstained side window of the wreckage. Everything is upturned, what do you see?

Note: this quick and easy imaginative paragraph is to be read aloud or pre-recorded, it is to be listened to as the stage of introspection becomes complete and one searches for the object of the meditation. This short meditation is designed to see how we all view death, and in particular the death of others. Some will see a horrible scene of decapitation and gore; others will see people in an unconscious, yet unharmed condition. This meditation is to see the way your mind works, especially in relation to death – good or bad!

SHRINKING

You see yourself shrink, getting smaller and smaller. The room in which you are presently in gets larger and larger as you become smaller and smaller. Eventually you are as small as a fly-speck and then smaller and then . . . .

Note: a simple guide to viewing the idea of diminishing into nothing and therefore dying. This should be accompanied by ideas of why, and how and what to do next? Finally, the question which arises is – what am I now that I am nothing?

THE TREE

Imagine in front of you a huge tree stem, so large that it obscures your vision either way you look, both left and right. It's height goes up forever and its depth goes down forever. Approach it, touch it with your hands, feel the bark and the life which flows through it. Grasp hold of the bark and the branches and climb, either up or down. Start to move from branch to branch in your chosen direction, moving slowly at first, and then as fast as you will, searching out the realms beyond life, travel where your will demands.

THE MOUND

You approach a mound, a grassy clump in the middle of a beech wood. You circle the mound and see an entrance, a hole with supporting stones; stones which look as if they were there from the beginning of time, before the primordial void gave way to the mist of the mother. See the entrance, dark and uninviting, go forward, examine the stone entrance, look at them, see the markings engraved by the hand of some pagan past; spirals and swastikas, bird's feet patterns. Now go in, reach within the darkness, enter the cool and damp air of the mound, see what lies before you. Chambers of rock, solid stone and dirt, shadows approach you in the looming light. Nothing is real, all unreal, reach forward, take the hand of darkness, go on, grasp the hand, it won't bite, take it! The cold hand guides you deeper into the rocky, cool interior of the mound, deeper, on into the ground you go, guided by the hand of darkness, follow quickly, journey where you will.

Note: The meditation, as The Tree, is to be continued by the meditator, it is his own dark unconscious mind, symbol of death, which he/she is to uncover. They will search for symbols and everything they create out of either the darkness or the two paths of the Tree will be significant to the evaluation of their own minds. Trips like this, which lead into the unknown and are then stopped, can be seen to be a trip into the unknown aspects of the mind. Likewise one could use such symbols as a cave mouth or perhaps a steel ladder into the sky or down into a sewer. The following is similar to this idea.

THE DARKNESS OF THE VOID

Before you is the light, pure, white, radiant light, surrounding all that is. No landscape, no contours or shapes, sounds or smells, just pure white light and life. Beyond, in the distance, appears a speck, a black speck. It travels towards you, closer and closer until it is blotting out the light and taking over. Into the dark you go, the light has gone, only darkness remains, the darkness of yourself. What do you see, feel, taste and sense in this darkness?

Death Play ; There are other ways of experiencing death. Plays can be enacted and visualization used in conjunction to enliven the proceedings. The modern cults of witchcraft use this in their initiation; the candidate is flung into the circle, blindfolded. This is a shove into the unknown, the dark and death. The hidden aspects of our mind, as we saw a little earlier, also represent death. This form of play, with the unknown is a form of death. The witchcraft intiation is therefore guite a good representation of death; if, and only if, the initiate does not know what is comng next. Likewise, darkness and solitude represent the same.

Word Play can also, when used in connection with meditation, bring about a link with death thought. In a circle of friends, sitting in their meditation postures, pass words around with the thought of death. Start with death and go from there. Something like this will emerge; death, dark, darkness, night, the moon, waning, the void, and beyond, evil, blood, sacifice, head, horns, animal, mind, the unconscious etc. The words can go in a specific order, clockwise, or more appropriately, counter-clockwise. The words can also take on the form of the void, chaotic; that is everyone shouting simultaneously that which they feel in connection with their own thought chain.

Another form of death meditation can be that of a sort of *Godform Assumption*. This can take on many different manners; taking up their positions in meditation, meditating upon a pictoral representation of them, chanting their names in a mantra etc. This here would obviously take the form of the Dread Lord or the Dark Goddess. I use a method of open-eye meditation, incorporating a mask. I make the mask out of paper-maché and paint either a picture of the God or symbols representative of the God. I then, in the meditative position, gaze upon myself in the mirror. For death, I use the mask of the void, of the power working behind all creation; that of Wyrd. In this manner one sees oneself as the mandala upon which oneself gazes.

The Mask of Wyrd

Day-Dream Imagination; Another idea, that of a day-dream type pathworking can also be useful to penetrate the depths of darkness. I usually prefer to use a myth or legend which already has certain geographical signposts for the use of the mind. In this way, the mind can travel through an already recognisable and powerful scenery. The Greek Underworld is one which would perhaps fit the bill well. The signposts are there, to death, the river Styx, the ferry-man Charon to whom a gold coin must be paid, Hermes the guide, Cerberus the three-headed guardian of the Underworld, the crossroads and the three paths of choice, those of the norm being the Asphodel fields, Tartarus for the wicked and Elysium for the good. In this way a day-dream can turn into a real soul journey if applied with the delving concentrative meditation technique.

Many images still remain and it is only one's own creativeness which will bring them to fruition. Likewise, I don't expect any of the ideas I have mentioned to work, at least not on their own. They must be given the power and inspiration of the soul. Only through creative working can one experience. The first time you try and visualize the Dakini stripping the flesh from your soul-skeleton you will not have the capacity, perhaps, to fully develop the experience. Eliade says, as does Huxley, that these experiences are sought after, they are sought after much searching, deprivation and silence. Likewise the technique must be correct and to a stage of some advance if we are to gain anything. But, through constant trying, effort and practice, perhaps one day the Dakini really will strip away the facade of your ego and reveal the pure soul and the light behind the third eye of Kali.

KALI

This meditation can be used in conjunction with an open-eye technique using an image of Kali as the focus of concentration. The idea is to see behind the mask. If one is in a group, it is a good idea after the meditation to express and relate emotions and scenes which occured and discuss connections and differences. A mantra may also be used, perhaps the Goddess's name; "Kali Ma", over and over again. This will have to be used by the whole group aloud or singular individuals silently.

Approach Kali, Goddess of Death. See her, dark and dim; skin as black and blue as bile. Her hair in a tangled mess resembling black snakes. She stands over a corpse – you. She jumps up and lands on your chest, crushing it in the process. Your eyes almost pop out of your skull as the pressure of her weight mounts. She is laughing, laughing at you.

See the necklace she wears, it is made of skulls, the skulls of the dead, perhaps your skull will soon join that which hang upon the thread. She waves the sacrificial knife above her head, holding a freshly severed head in one of her other four arms. Flesh quivers in the other hand, a blackbird picks at it, its beak dripping thick congealing blood.

You watch as she dances, dances the dances of death upon your body, all you can do is watch, she raises the sword and aims it at your skull, you know the following, it slices down and severs your head with a piercing blow, crushing your neck bones and freeing your head from your body.

She picks the head up by the hair, and holds it in front of her own

44

Kali

face, gazing into your eyes and laughing, you see too into hers and watch her third eye, the eye in the centre of the forehead, you watch in a hypnotic trance as you enter it. Your final moments of living consciousness are spent contemplating it, you begin too, to enter it. Getting closer and closer to the eye. The eye, which is as black as pitch. Into it you go, into the enveloping darkness behind the eye, into the darkness of death, keep going and discover death.

Note: The meditator should be enraptured by the vision of Kali and likewise death. He thus enters, after being killed, the third eye of Kali, into the very mind of death, into the realm of the beyond. There the meditator is left to discover in a personal pathworking climax. The meditator can in no way be led to the end of death by direction alone, he/she can only be introduced to it and then their own minds must take control and chase the image of death unto its final realization. After some time has elapsed the meditator should be brought out, either by the soothing voice of the pathworker or his own mind; which ever is the first.

CLASSICAL TIBETAN

Whilst Kali is the death aspect and also the rebirth aspect of life and is commonly seen to be the destroyer in these meditations, there is also a Goddess or rather Goddesses called Dakinis. These are the helpers of the dying and can be either fierce or gentle. The fierce ones are those like the one we are about to encounter; the gentle ones are those who help the dead and the dying. Their abodes are seen as cemeteries and as such, as the image of death, they are a part of the Kali Goddess. They also, like Kali, have a necklace of skulls, usually they also carry the sacrificial sword and a bowl in the other hand. They are also seen as "the female who gives wisdom through initiation". As we have already demonstrated, the real wisdom, is that of death.

Imagine yourself as a corpse. A white (or black of course) corpse, lying quietly upon the ground. All is still. Even the wind does not rustle the reeds. A howling pierces the air, and a dancing figure approaches the corpse, the howling increasing in intensity, the corpse lies still. Now in front of the body a Dakini stands, raging and wailing, the smell of rotten flesh accompanies her. See her raise the blade of sacrifice in the air, high above her head, waiting to drop. Suddenly the blade falls, slicing off your head. Watch as the blood gushes forth from the gaping neck wound, the head rolls along the ground, eventually to be picked up by the Dakini.

She now begins to strip away your flesh, piece by piece, wrenching it away from the muscle. The veins and sinew tear. Utter agony and despair overwhelm you in this process. Imagine the separation of the skin from the flesh, the flesh from the muscle, the muscle from the bones. She tears the pieces up and throws them to the void, you watch as creatures of every sort feast on your flesh, chewing at the quivering and glistening morsels of warm flesh, still oozing with blood, red blood, all is red.

Your skeleton remains, white like the glare of the mid-day sun. Now she takes your skin and stretches it like a drum skin across the third void and beyond. You are covering all that there is in the universe, all life with your death, and still your skeleton remains, all white, bleached and clean, all blood and sinew gone. Contemplate your skeleton, watch it, all the bones that lie there in an organised heap, watch them.

The Dakini gathers together all the skin now and the remaining flesh and blood. She wraps it in the stretched skin and makes a parcel which she dashes upon the rocks and pulps into an unrecognisable glob of entrails. You are this mass, you are this skin and bone, see the pulp and see yourself, see your skeleton and see yourself, there still remains your skeleton, white and gleaming in the mid-day sun, you still remain.

Note: It is totally necessary to realise what is happening and to be in a deep form of meditation where the happenings are imagined as real. You must experience the tearing and rippng, feel it in the very depths of your being. The picture must be clear and vivid, as must the remaining skeleton which is the clue to the whole process, and the key to the soul. It is not necessarily the ripping apart that matters, but rather the image of a terrifying death, something which appears as the worst of the worst of nightmares. You must transcend and experience everything as real, as having been killed and resurrected. This meditation is really in the order of initiation; the resurrection however is seen as your return to ordinary consciousness. You have experienced death and come back to tell the tale. This need not be a pathworking but rather it can be read through initially and then pictured in the mind later when the correct stage of meditation has been reached. One can supplement this by using it perhaps in a graveyard or alone in the wilderness where there is a sense of loss and loneliness.

Likewise one can use the Eskimo meditation where the Great Bear of the Lakes comes out and devours you. Feel its jaws close around you, feel the flesh being ripped off, strip after strip until nothing remains apart from the bleached skeleton. In the Eskimo meditation they then see the bones being taken apart and then placed back together again in the same order, but with a name for each bone. Do this in your own mind; watch as the bones are taken, named and replaced.

As I mentioned earlier, in relation to the use of psychedelics and the *Bardo Thodol,* Tim Leary produced a book as a guide. This guide is for use with L.S.D. and the taker is to read chapters and 'experience' certain or all parts of the death, vision and rebirth states of death. These can, and have, been used successfully in meditation as a guide, in a pathworking manner, to the death experience. For this reason I here include his pathworking poem which introduces the first bardo, that is an introduction to death. This first poem can be read at the onset of a death meditation experience, with the group already past the pratyahara stage and working with dharana. The second meditation which I give is Leary's poem on Illusion, the third being a meditation of the void. These he uses to prevent re-entry, I use them as a stimulus for the mind to contact aspects of death. The first I believe to be extremely useful, as a guide, pathworking and meditation.

First Bardo Instruction

The time has come for you to seek new levels of reality.
Your ego and the (name) game are about to cease.
You are about to be set face to face with the clear light.
You are about to experience it in its reality.
In the ego-free state, whereas all things are like the void and cloudless
    sky,
And the naked spotless intellect is like a transparent vacuum;
At this moment, know yourself and abide in that state.

O (name of the voyager),
That which is called ego-death is coming to you.
Remember:
This is now the hour and death of rebirth;
Take advantage of this temporary death to obtain the perfect state –
    Enlightment.
Concentrate on the unity of all living beings.
Hold on to the Clear Light.
Use it to attain understanding and love.
If you cannot maintain bliss of illumination and if you are slipping back
    into contact with the external world,
Remember:
The hallucinations which you may now experience,
The visions and insights,
Will teach you much about yourself and the world.
The veil of routine perception will be torn from your eyes.
Remember the unity of all living things.
Remember the bliss of the Clear Light.
Let it guide you through the visions of this experience.
Let it guide you through your new life to come.
If you feel confused; call upon the memory of your friends and the
    power of the person whom you most admire.

O (name),
Try to reach and keep the experience of the Clear Light.
Remember:
The light is the life energy.

The endless flame of life.
An ever-changing surging turmoil of color may engulf your vision.
This is the ceaseless transformation of energy.
The Life process.
Do not fear it.
Surrender to it.
Join it.
It is part of you.
You are part of it.
Remember also:
Beyond the restless flowing electricity of life is the ultimate reality –
    The Void.
Your own awareness, not formed into anything possessing form or
    color, is naturally void.
The final reality.
The All Good.
The All Peaceful.
The light.
The Radiance.
The movement is the fire of life from which we all come.
Join it.
It is part of you.
Beyond the light of life is the peaceful silence of the void.
The quiet bliss beyond all transformations.
The Buddha smile.
The Void is beginning and end itself.
Unobstructed; shining, thrilling, blissful.
Diamond consciousness.
The All-Good Buddha.
Your own consciousness, not formed into anything.
No thought, no vision, no color, is void.
The intellect shining and blissfully silent –
This is the state of perfect enlightment.
Your own consciousness, shining, void and inseperable from the great
    body of radiance, has no birth, nor death.
It is the immutable light which the Tibetans call Buddha Amitabha,
The awareness of the formless beginning.
Knowing this is enough.

Recognize the voidness of your own consciousness to be Buddhahood. Keep this recognition and you will maintain the state of the divine mind of the Buddha.

MEDITATION ON ILLUSIONS

The sexual activities, the manipulation machinery, the mocking
    laughter, dashing sounds of terrifying apparitions,
Indeed all phenomena.
Are in their nature, illusions.
However they may appear, in truth, they are unreal and fake.
They are like dreams and apparitions.
Non-permanent, non-fixed.
What advantage is there in being attached to them,
Or being afraid of them?
The mind itself does not exist,
Therefore why should they?
Only through taking these illusions for real will you wander around in
    this confused existence.
All these are like dreams,
Like echoes,
Like cities of clouds,
Like mirages,
Like mirrored forms,
Like phantasmagoria,
The moon seen in water.
Not real even for a moment.
By holding one pointedly to that train of thought.
The belief that they are real is dissipated,
And liberation is attained.

MEDITATION ON THE VOID

"All substances are part of my own consciousness.
This consciousness is vacuous, unborn, and unceasing."
Thus meditating,
Allow the mind to rest in the uncreated state.
Like the pouring of water into water,
The mind should be allowed its own easy mental posture.

In its natural, unmodified condition, clear and vibrant.
By maintaining this relaxed, uncreated state of mind
Rebirth into routine game-reality is sure to be prevented.
Meditate on this until you are certainly free.

Using these as guides to meditation, voidness and illusion, they may help the seeker along the path to death-experience realization. Although Leary's books were designed for L.S.D. and other hallucinogenic drugs, he did have insight into the meditational and 'ordinary consciousness' aspects of the 'game'. The poems and guide above quoted are from the book mentioned previously and are designed specifically around the *Bardo Thodol,* and therefore around the death and rebirth experience.

DEATHWORD

Death has been glimpsed not through the self but through the black print on the white paper; black and white, death and birth. There are many living in the world that have experienced death as a form of initiation. It is for the reader, or at least those interested, to take death by the balls and experience it as it should be; with the whole soul, egoless and naked.

Death will come, hopefully during life, in that way it will make better the time of physical death and perhaps an easier rebirth. Letting go of the mind and the personal self are the hardest thing a man or woman can do; yet it is all a man or woman can do to experience death and in turn – life.

ILLUSTRATIONS

1. Trappist Monk Meditating in Graveyard (pg 38). From *Manners and Customs of Mankind,* Ed. J.A. Harmnerton. Amalgamated Press, London.
2. Mask of Wyrd (pg 43). Author's collection. 1986.
3. Kali (pg 45) by Andy Langdel. 1987.

SOURCES

1. *Yoga-Sutra of Patanjali,* Dr. J.R. Ballantyne, Indological Press, 1971. Delhi.
2. *A Dictionary of Symbols,* Tom Chetwynd, Paladin Books, 1982.
3. *The Lord of the Dance,* Anthony Duncan, Helios, 1972.
4. *Shamanism: Archaic Techniques of Ecstasy,* M. Eliade Bollingen Series, 1974.
5. *The Tibetan Book of the Dead,* Dr. W.Y. Evans-Wentz, Oxford University, 1980.
6. *The Golden Bough,* J.G. Frazer; Macmillan Press, 1978.
7. *The Greek Myths: Vol. 1,* R. Graves, Pelican, 1969.
8. *The Way of the Sacred,* F. Huxley, Aldous Books Ltd., 1974.
9. *Psychedelic Experience,* T. Leary; Academy Editions, 1971.
10. *Tantra,* P. Rawson, Thames and Hudson, 1973.
11. *The Quest for Merlin,* N. Tolstoy, Hamish Hamilton, 1985.
12. *The Upanishads,* Trans. J. Mascaro, Penguin, 1981.
13. *The Woman's Encyclopedia of Myths and Secrets,* B. Walker, Harper & Row, 1983.
14. *The Romeo Error,* L Watson, Coronet, 1976.
15. *Death,* A. Watts, Celestial Arts, 1975.
16. *A Celtic Anthology,* G. Rhys; Harrap & Co., 1927.

www.ingramcontent.com/pod-product-compliance
Lightning Source LLC
Chambersburg PA
CBHW051739040426
42447CB00008B/1221